WEED

BLASPHEMY

EASTERN GLORY

WEED BLASPHEMY

WEED BLASPHEMY

Designed by gold media publications, Abuja Nigeria

Edited by Harry Nwafor

email

easterngloryworld@gmail.com

 Eastern glory

 @easternglory

Content

Acknowledgement

For contributions, criticism and

constructive advice, the author would like to thank the following; Harry Nwafor, Imonitie Aregbeyen, Victor Ejiofor, Fatai Sadiq, Samuel Ajoma and Narconon world Wide Network.

DISCLAIMER

This book does not in any form encourage

Or discourage the use of weed both recreationally, medically and other wise. Therefore precautionary

Measures should be taken before, during and after weeding.

Since the

Intoxicating effect will be either of advantage or

Disadvantage to the user and the society

At large.

Introduction

Due to the need to prevent the spread of STDs and unwanted pregnancy since sex cannot be completely stopped, condoms were created to help reduce and prevent it spread, so also this book titled **weed blasphemy** is the condom for weed consumption.

Since the discovery of weed in the early age, it increased the wealth of the user states industrially, economically and medically but since the new world began it use has increased more through recreational and social consumption, but this weed as it is called has ruined people's lives and has also made others stingingly rich.

Yet government of most nations believes that the use of this plant today has destroyed more lives than it has helped, so they tried to stop the use of this weed in so many ways they could. But the true is, this is never possible now.

So therefore it is important we know what this weed intoxication effect offers the weeder, and also know how to use this intoxicating effect properly to better of our lives.

01

What is weed?

The leaves which is the most recognizable and well-known aspect of the cannabis plant, have featured in our artwork for thousands of years, from regions as disparate as Japan to Egypt. Despite the great degree of variation found naturally in local populations of cannabis, the leaves do not alter greatly in appearance between varieties.

Cannabis which is the name of the plant that provides weed might not be as popular as the word weed or marijuana. The word marijuana comes from Mexican Spanish, but the reason for this name is not clear. The leaves, flower, stem and other parts of the cannabis plant is what is been consumed as weed.

According to the standard phyllotaxy (the arrangement of leaves on a plant stem), cannabis leaves are compound (with multiple leaflets, as opposed to simple, where a single leaf grows from the stem) and decussate-opposite rather than alternate. Opposite leaves emerge in pairs, one each side of the stem, with a clear vertical space between the leaf pairs.

Decussate leaves are opposite, but each new leaf pair is at a right-angle to the last pair. Alternate leaves emerge from the stem singly, swapping sides as the vertical height increases.

02

Brief History about Cannabis (weed)

Thousands of years before the illicit drug industry in the Americas, the cannabis plant was used medicinally and industrially. For more than 3,000 years, it has been known that cannabis fibers were strong and durable, and provided excellent raw materials for cord and rope.

In ancient China and Egypt, cannabis (weed) was used medicinally for soreness from gout, rheumatism and other problems. The ancient Greeks also used cannabis to relieve inflammation.

When cannabis plants were used for fiber, ropes and clothes, the plant is referred to as hemp. The Chinese used hemp fibers for fabric and ropes starting as far back as 1000 BC. Fishing nets were also made of hemp. The world's oldest piece of paper dates back to around 500 BC and was made of hemp fibers. There was no cotton used in China until around 900 AD, increasing the importance of hemp.

While the intoxicating ingredients of cannabis are very low when the plant is cultivated in the best manner to produce clothing or rope, there is evidence that the ancient Chinese knew about this effect of the plant. Around 100 AD, a medical reference book stated that if the seeds were taken in excess, it "will produce hallucinations." The seeds were later mixed with wine to create an anesthetic that could be used during surgery.

The Romans and Vikings began to use hemp fibers for ropes. Both cultures relied heavily on sailing ships for exploration, colonization and trade. They lived or died by the ropes securing their sails. If ropes broke during a storm, the ship could be lost.

Much of the hemp used by the Romans was cultivated in Sicily. The Arabs had brought hemp seeds to Sicily, after using the plant for medicine, rope and cloth for hundreds of years.

Hemp ropes and fabrics continued to be used in Italy for centuries, particularly around Venice. Venice was known for its beautiful fabrics made of hemp, that were very long lasting and nearly as lovely as those made of silk. The Venetian hemp industry was competitive and highly regulated. Different regions around Venice produced hemp fibers of varying grades so the fibers were carefully labeled as to their origins. Hemp ropes also contributed to the superiority of the commercial ships carrying Venetian commodities to other parts of the world.

Gradually, the use of hemp moved to England, which became a major sea power around 1500 AD. King Henry VIII greatly increased the number of ships in the English navy and ordered that more cannabis or hemp be planted to provide the ropes for these ships. For various reasons,

English farmers could not meet the demand for hemp and so country began to import the fiber from Russia. England put great effort into maintaining their supplies of hemp as their trade and colonization activities in the Seventeenth and Eighteenth Centuries required the construction and maintenance of hundreds of ships.

03

Types of weed

Although cannabis leaves are usually decussate, as the plant prepares to flower the leaves may begin to emerge in an alternate pattern. Interestingly, rejuvenated cannabis plants demonstrate alternate phyllotaxy. Experiments with hemp showed that early-planted specimens, which flowered in low light conditions but did not die, began to put out new alternate leaf growth when hours of sunlight increased. The initial new growth was simple rather than compound, and as new growth continued, the number of leaflets gradually increased.

There is some evidence that this phenomenon leads to vegetative growth of greatly increased vigour, although the genetic processes responsible are not fully understood. It is thought that the evolution of opposite-decussate phyllotaxy occurred comparatively recently, from an alternate-leaved ancestor, and that the genes controlling the decussate phyllotaxy 'switch off' around the time of inflorescence.

Putting aside the eccentricities of cannabis leaf growth for a moment, let us take a look at the differences between the three main subspecies of cannabis. Firstly, sativa the leaves are long and slender, often with pronounced serrations, giving the leaves a jagged, almost spiky appearance. The coloration of sativa leaves ranges from bright, lime green to blackish-green at the darkest. The largest leaves can often have up to thirteen leaflets. Secondly, indica its leaves are much wider, and the largest leaves usually have fewer leaflets than the largest sativa leaves, at seven to nine leaflets. Indica leaves are commonly deep olive-green; very light green leaves are rare and often a sign of deficiency.

Thirdly is the ruderalis which leaves are generally smaller than the other subspecies', as the mature plant is much smaller overall, and the largest leaves may contain anything from five to thirteen leaflets. Ruderalis leaves are usually closer to the indica in terms of width, although they can be much narrower than any indica leaf would normally be.

The main intoxicating ingredient in weed is known as THC which is DELTA-9-TETRAHYDROCANNABINOL. Since the discovery of this ingredient, farmer has tried to use various growing process to grow the plant, and these has given it a different quality of THC. Since the involvement of farmers into the different growing processes, this has brought about the different types of weed. Different other types of intoxicating effect have been gotten through different processes of mixing weed with different substances before taken. Here are few of them if you might want to know:

1. Skunk: a particular kind of marijuana often grown hydroponically

2. Weed that are mixed with spirit or vodka and dried up for smoking. This type don't have a definite name

3. Weed mixed with other leaves like pawpaw and lemon grass, for smoking

4. Weed poured into bottle filled with dry gin, and been drank after several days.

5. Sinsemilla (a particular type of marijuana involving use of only female plants)

6. Hash: a particular preparation of marijuana resin.

7.   Blunts   (cigars   filled   with marijuana).

8.   Weed is also cooked with food.

 Since the use of this drug increased, different user country, groups and sect of different works of life now have code names and slangs for it. Most of these names have gone viral, According   to   the   US   Drug Enforcement   Administration;   these are the terms commonly used for marijuana:

Aunt Mary, BC Bud, Boom, Chronic, Dope, Gangster, Ganja, Grass Herb, Hydro, Indo, Joint, Kif, Mary Jane, Mota, Pot, Reefer, Smoke, Weed,

Yerb. These are other names referred to weed by Nigerians; ibo, kalaku. jelousin, feel alright, nnwayi ocha, kpoli, human grass and so on.

04

13 Laws of Weed

Most tools, items, gadgets or drugs purchased from a retail shop worldwide usually come with a safety guide caution leaflet attached to it. Weed which is not an exception has now gotten its own. So therefore every weeder or an intending weeder must adhere to this laws strictly before, during and after weeding, to avoid been discriminated against, insulted, looked down at or arrested as the case may be.

1 . A weeder must know his or her limit or gauge

2 . A weeder must make sure there is readily available food to eat after weeding. This is very important because the weed works with the nervous system, which immediately tells the weeder it's time to eat.

3 . A weeder must not pass weed to someone who do not ask for it. This is because some people might see it irritating, if the rolled up paper is soaked with saliva. (b) it might be a way of influencing the person into the habit of constant weeding.

4 . A weeder must be sure the weeding environment is safe and friendly enough to weed.

5 . Weed should not be sold to persons under the age of 18.

6 . A weeder must not always beg for weed. If the intending weeder can't afford it, then it should be disdained. But if the intending weeder still wants to keep up with weeding, the previous weed the weeder took should have given the weeder an idea on how to make money positively in other to constantly afford it.

7 . A weeder should constantly wash his or her mouth well after weeding, this is because the odor might be very offensive to some people when perceived and it may give them a bad impression about you.

8. A weeder must not engage in any form of negative activities that may cause lost of life and property after weeding.

9 . Know your right mood and time of weeding.

10 . Do not weed with strangers.

11 . A weeder must not weed a rolled up stuff he is not sure of what the content is.

12. A weeder must not weed with the intension of impressing his fellow weeders and others.

13 . Always puff and pass the weed on time if you are weeding with understanding friends, don't hog it.

05

Weed blasphemy

Since we may have understood the laws of weed, the types and various names that it is called. It will be very important for you the reader to understand what blasphemy means which is the main reason why this book was written.

Blasphemy is the act of insulting something or someone or exhibiting an action that can be insulting to people or a religious believe. While Weed Blasphemy is the process of displaying or exhibiting an unpleasant character or engaging in a negative and unaccepted societal behavior that could cause lost of life and property or could lead to set back morally, mentally, physically and economically after weeding.

 Weed is a sacred plant that could develop the weeder's mind by increasing the weeder's wisdom, knowledge, and understanding and also gives the weeder a deep thinking ability.

This book Weed blasphemy will be incomplete without explaining this self discovered theory about weed which states that **'once a weeder takes weed, the weeder has**

automatically stepped into the room filled with both good and bad abundance opportunity and goals easy achieving formula at the weeder's disposal'.

But Most times the made available good formulas are not followed because of daily life distractions and also because weeders have not been properly sensitized about the benefits and proper usage of weed intoxicating effect, which can only be felt when a weeder weed's or sometimes be intoxicated in weed like drug or sometimes alcohol. But the biggest problems a common weeder have, is the inability to choose and follow a positive dreams formula instead of a less important and negative dreams the mostly go for when intoxicated. A perfect example of this is a weeder who after weeding gets inspired to kill for monetary benefit, religious or spiritual reasons. This is a negative form of confident, opportunity and motivation that the room offers the weeder.

Every weeder who are all above the age of accountability, and surely knows what good and bad is, should program their minds to choose and adhere to the positive easy dreams actualizing formula after stepping into the room of various dreams opportunity were the door was opened by weed intoxication.

Actions that blasphemes weed

By displaying a negative character that was chosen in the room were the door was open by weed intoxication, or in other words displaying attitudes and character that are questionable, disgusting and might lead to lost of life and property or living a life that might make a weeder to be looked down at and discriminated against or by living a life due to ones weeding habit that does not make the weeder better off than when he was not weeding, that weeder is seen as a weed blasphemer. It is often easy for one to be a blasphemer.

Weed has the ability to control the weeder's mind and thought, if the weeder do not understand weed intoxicating effect, and has not embark on the journey of self discovery, which is advised for every weeder to undergo. The weeder must be positive minded, and know how to concentrate weed intoxicating effect into something positively beneficial to the weeder, family and the world at large.

There are thousands of way that a weeder can be a weed blasphemer unconsciously and might not know, here are few of them

1. Weeding in other to deliberately do evil.

2 . Encouraging someone who has never tasted weed to do so.

3. Constantly using weed intoxicating effect for sleeping. Someone who is struggling financially and is living below poverty line should not use weed as sleeping medicine, it should be used for brainstorming, imagining and executing mind blowing task and idea that will change the weeder's life.

4 . Weeding in an uncondusive and unfavorable place. A weeder can

avoid this type of blasphemy if he weedes in his house or club were weed is allowed.

5 . A weeder has blasphemed weed if he weeds without an available food to eat after weeding.

6 . So many weeders today always have thousands of reasons they think it's positive enough for them to continue weeding and are ready to die convincing people that is it. But truly it is insanity for a weeder to continue weeding always without experiencing or achieving any positive result. But if the weeder's conscience is dead that he cannot

see he is blaspheming then he should be encourage enrolling for conscience awakening class.

7 . A weeder must not weed in the present of people who see weeders as bad people.

8 . Lastly, weeder who might go against the 13 laws of weed is weed blasphemers.

06

Uses of weed intoxicating effect

A man once said, 'eat what is good for you', and good here means what adds value to you either socially, mentally or medically. Also good here might be what increases the growth and development of your mind and social well being. In other words, that saying means one should equally disease from whatever he consumes that is not good for him. Since the increase in social consciousness in our present day, people began to see weed as a must take drug. Because of the way is it been openly displayed in music video and social gatherings, Many believes it gives a kind of bad boy looks and confident that we believe everybody should have a bit of, because the bad boy character is more entertaining and always remembered than that of a humbly good one. By so doing, freshers and some so called weeders unconsciously gave their self to be used by weed.

According to a Morgan freeman film Lucy, a CPH 4 drugs was implanted inside Lucy's and three others for exporting. Those drugs made her to be able to use 100percent of her brain functional ability after she retrieved and ingested the three other dosages adding to the one that busted inside her.

This justifies the fact that drugs like weed also has a positive effect if used properly. We also see the aspect of her using that ability to diagnose her sister's sickness and immediately prescribed a drug for her to take, and didn't use that ability to do evil or negative things that many people with such ability would rather do.

Secondly, according to the thriller movie "Limitless," a writer who takes an experimental drug known as NZT48 allows him to use 100 percent of his brain, providing him with superhuman memory, psychic power, concentration, and other fantastic abilities.

For great movie directors to come up with this idea about drug use to enhancing brain power and other related films. That's a prove that weed or weed like drug are used sometimes by most successful professionals movie directors for perfect imaging and script writing. Lastly, most successful risk takers, inventors, business men, pilots, entertainers and scholars from early age till now all have a trace of weed in their DNAs, and have made great use of its intoxicating effect without blaspheming it. And yet, are still been respected and looked up to, till today believe it or not. Here are few of them; you can research about after reading this book:

Joan of Arc, Alexander Duman, Queen Victoria, William Shakespeare, George Washington, Christopher Columbus, Hau Tuo, Abdulaziz 1, Elizabeth 1, William Broke Oshaughnessy, John F. Kenedy, Morgan Freeman, Jay Z, bob Marley, Steve jobs, the Beatles, Rihanna, Wiz Kid, Rick Ross, Abraham Lincoln, Bill Gate and Cameron Diaz. The list is endless.

You might also be shocked that most successful people you admire around you are weeder, but you hardly know because they don't blasphem it.

Many people believe we only use a small fraction of our brain before we die, some people even claim that they are able to use more of their brains than others,

After all, who knows what we could do by tapping into the other 80 or 90 percent we're not using? If you weeder feels you've only accessed 20 percent of your brains... well, weed might lets you access all of it!

That's the promise if only you don't blaspheme it.

07

Mental or physical problems
caused by weeding

According to World Drug Report, cannabis products can produce temporary symptoms of psychosis, loss of ability to learn or remember recent events, reduced ability to carry out certain mental tasks, make certain decisions and pay attention.

There is a growing body of evidence that suggests that a person who starts using cannabis early and uses is heavily could run an increased risk of psychotic disorders.

Physically, marijuana smokers have risks similar to those of smokers: bronchitis, emphysema, asthma. Extensive use can cause suppression of the immune system and can increase the risk of cancer to the head, neck and lungs.

A report in Spain stated that they had found a link between heavy marijuana use and psychosis that starts during adolescence. Researchers ruled out any connection to use of other drugs.

But the name of the successful weeder listed above has rubbished most of our medical report to some extent, because at a point the world centers on making money and being successful. But if you believe in the medical reports and you want to stop weeding without haven't visualized and made proper use of weed intoxicating effect then you must be the world greatest fool alive.

08

Reasons why weeders are been discriminated against

One of the most troubling aspects of current marijuana policy in most country, even in those states that have legalized marijuana, is the continuing job discrimination faced by those who smoke weed.

For instant in some states around the world, a private employer is legally free to fire anyone who tests positive for THC in their system, without the slightest suggestion the individual came to work in an impaired condition. It is a relic left over from the "reefer madness" days when marijuana smokers were considered bad people, and employers were anxious to identify smokers and get rid of them.

Arizona and other states does not permit employers to discriminate against legal medical marijuana users (they do not yet have legal recreational use) "unless a failure to do so would cause an employer to lose a monetary or licensing benefit under federal law or regulations." Of course, but employees in this marijuana legalize states are not protected if they come to work in an impaired condition, or possess or use marijuana in the workplace. Until we manage to change federal law, that is a good model for new states to consider, as they draft either medical use or full legalization proposals.

Secondly, in Africa weeders also face discrimination in schools, were they are been considered as cultist or bad gang members by their course mates and lectures. Weeders are also believed to be the group of people responsible for protest or agitating in school for proper student welfare like increase of school fee and dilapidated class rooms renovation among others. This is because the governing body of the school thinks weed somehow gives confident to the populated introvert student to take up the street not minding the danger. Forgetting that the people's right cannot be deprived off them without them protesting.

There are hundreds of events and places that weeders are been discriminated and this is because weed or cannabis as it is called still has a status of bad and illegal in the people's eyes.

 Lastly, the major reason that makes weeders to be generally discriminated against is because of the attitude of sellout blasphemers who never do anything positively meaningful with weed intoxicating effect.

9

Story of a repented weed blasphemer

In an eastern state of Nigeria lay a town named Umunze .From where a young man named Obi Agu was born in the 90s.From his early age he had in mind what he wanted in life which was money fame and power which were inseparable to him. He did part of his primary school in the north then went to his hometown to stay with his grandmother were he completed his basic six because she was lonely and sick and needed someone to stay with. His grand mom was a hard working woman who became very popular because of her generosity, peace loving and constantly agitating for women's true rights, but she was an addicted snuff sniffer. Growing up with his grand mom was kind of bored for him because he hardly knew his neighbor and he had no friends to play with. But as time goes on he began to find the place interesting. He constantly wondered why his grand mom was so influential so he didn't hesitate to ask her, but she constantly gave him no answer and always asks him to try to understand himself. Obi Agu was always confuse any time she said that, but he kept asking never minding if she would answer or not, but little Obi Agu never knew he was too young to understand. He grew up becoming hard working, industrious, and multi talented. Even his grand mom wandered how Obi Agu can do virtually everything he saw someone do .After about two years later when Obi Agu had gained admission into secondary school, on a Saturday evening she sent him on an errand to buy snuff, he was shocked and confused because that was the first time she ever send him on such errands. He did not know what to do, because he believes it wasn't right to buy snuff and was also bad to disobey elders, so he immediately told her he wanted to use the toilet.

So that he could talk to his mind to be convinced of weather to go or not, then he remember his teacher popular saying he had made his favorite 'there is a price to pay for every greatness'. He immediately came out and collected the money and left. That evening when he came back, she prepared his favorite dish and after eating, while she was taking her snuff she open up her secrete of inspiration and what made her influential. Many success key was given to Obi Agu that night and indeed the answer to his longed asked question. And this was the answer 'intoxication effect is a privilege to those who feels it, use it positively well to your advantage. It was indeed a long memorable night he never forgot .It took obi several days of deep research and reading to fully understand what his grand mom meant by that phrase. And from that moment Obi Agu, changed his perception about drug users generally and began to make friends with them. Without time wasting obi had became a weeder, at first he was hiding it from his grand mom and people, but he never knew that weeder who don't have understanding of weed are often been controlled and misled by it. In couple of months obi couldn't hide it any longer because the negative signs were all over him by the way he dresses, talks and behave. His mouth was constantly smelling weed and he was daily looking malnourished because be barely go home. shortly obi began picking pocket and stealing to get money to buy weed, he was also committing all forms of criminal behavior and causing unrest in his neighborhood, school and every were he goes. Obi quickly forgot his dreams and thought he has actualized it by misunderstanding it with the kind of life he is was currently living. He was arrested several times and beaten up by group of people when caught committing any criminal act, which is the most synonymous character of premature mind weeders. Obi was enlisted in the black book of his school and parent seriously began to discipline their children when they were seen talking to obi. Obi finally completed his secondary education and his character was going from worst to worst daily, he engaged in greater dubious act like raping girls, stealing high voltage wire and insulators. His community got tired of his characters and planed with the police that he should be shot to dead if caught performing any of his trade. He immediately travelled out of his state when he had about it.

On a fateful night obi and two of his friends mounted a road block on a major road in rivers state of Nigeria, to steal from travelers and those who were returning from work at that time of the night. Obi was holding a toy gun while his two friends were handling locally made guns loaded with few bullets. Obi was full of confident that he never mind evening performing the operation without any weapon as he has always done, shortly as usual the operation began, one of his friend was the one holding the bag for collecting money and other useful items from their victims. The operation was suppose to last for 1hour but in 20 mint time the police were already present, the shot his two friend, and Obi luckily escaped into the bush with a bullet wound on his right hand, he kept running deep into the bush quietly without any vision of where he was going. The police chased him for some distance and went back, believing that they might have shot him to dead when they opened fire at different directions of the bush while they were chasing him. Obi then stopped under a big tree to rest. After a while he discovered a small wet side bag on the ground close to where he was sitting. He thought it might be money left by another group of thieves. Then he touched his pocket to know if his small touch light phone was still with him, it was there..... He removed it, and flashed the touch inside the bag and behold it was a wet book titled THE JOURNEY CALLED YOU written by Julie Luimano, He disappointingly took the book and came very close to the road side from a different direction. He waited for day to break while he managed to stop the bleeding wound with leaves he plugged from the bush.

At around 5 am he came out, flanged down a trailer and told the driver he was traveling to Anambra luckily for him the trailer was traveling that direction. He pleaded with them and lied that he had been attacked by arm robbers, and the pitied him and gave him a ride.

He entered the trunk of the trailer and shortly slept off; he slept off and woke up when he heard noise around him. He was home, he quickly jumped down and thanked the driver and went his way. He took a bike straight to his house, without talking to anybody entered his room, took his only 5 thousand naira he has miraculously saved and asked the bike man to take him to a chemist outside his town. Obi pays the bike man and went into the chemist to be treated. He came out bought some food to eat, then he went back home, took his bath and entered his room to read the book he believes was somehow kept in the bush for him. After flipping pages of the book to find the most interesting part he came to it.

After reading that part, he came back to the beginning to start from scratch. Obi couldn't finish the book because he was a slow reader, but that moment he remembered his grand mom saying,

'UNDERSTAND YOUR SELF' the answer she usually gave him when he asked what made her influential. Indeed he now understands himself and realized the shame he had caused his grand mom. He asked his grand mom for forgiveness and promised to be useful to himself.

From that day Obi Agu stop being a weed blasphemer and began to produce and package a local beverage even better than what his town people travel long distance to buy .He continued weeding and got ideas on how to produce a rich chocolate flavored drink which was better than most foreign chocolate drinks. Shortly his product became very popular; he became rich and became one of his town's successful people.

10

Conclusion

If you have tried to do something positively useful after weeding, or have tried to brain storm new ideas and be innovative for you to be useful in your society and your brain is failing to, but instead it is doing the opposite, then quiet weeding. It is not your thing, after all a man's food, to another it is poison.

A weeder must be opened minded towards learning new things and accepting his short comings, in other to be corrected and avoid being a blasphemer.

A weeder must study to be intelligent if he really wants to make a proper use of weed intoxicating effect, because it is sometimes difficult for an illiterate to make a good use of most amazing ideas popped up by weed intoxicating effect.

All weeder who follow the positive easy goal achieving formula gotten from weed intoxicating effect without an atom of blasphemy are driving toward greatness and will arrive there in no time. Then after the weeder have achieved this, in no time there won't be stoppage, penalizing and discriminating against the weeder for weeding, because the weeder would have contributed his own quota towards developing his country in his own small way.

Then the government won't hesitate to diversify the money used for destroying weed farms and prosecuting weeders for further weed sensitization programs and improving the lives of the citizens, and infrastructural facilities of the country.

Key words

Weeder: A weeder is a person that use
weed, either through smoking, cooking or
drinking.

Weed: Weed is marijuana or whatever
name you might call it.

Weed blasphemy: Weed Blasphemy is the
act of displaying or exhibiting an
unpleasant character or engaging in a
negative and unaccepted societal behavior
that could cause lost of life and property
and could lead to set back morally,
mentally, physically and economically
after weeding.

About the author

Eastern glory is a successful social crusader, human rights activist and a prolific writer. He is also the team leader of Big Dreams Support Group (BDSG). He is currently the Brand and Marketing Manager at theasisx ltd.